FLORIDA OUTHOUSES

FLORIDA OUTHOUSES

An Ode to the Shack in the Back

KEVIN McCARTHY

THE History PRESS

Published by The History Press
Charleston, SC 29403
www.historypress.net

Cover image: An outhouse near Citra. *Photo by the author*.

Unless otherwise noted, all photographs were taken by the author.

First published 2007

Manufactured in the United States

ISBN 978.1.59629.283.3

Library of Congress CIP data applied for.

Introduction

As a linguist interested in all parts of our language, I have always been fascinated by our reluctance to talk about the two most important events in our lives (birth and death) and the bodily functions we perform every day (urination and defecation). Another favorite topic of mine is Floridiana: anything related to the culture, history, customs and language of this, the fourth largest state in the nation.

The 2000 census, for example, indicated that some 21,400 homes in Florida lacked complete plumbing. Did some of those homes have working outhouses? If so, how could I find them? As I traveled throughout the state on research and lecture trips, I found many of them: abandoned ones on farms, restored ones in state parks, fake ones in gardens and, yes, functioning ones in place of indoor bathrooms.

I present the following pictorial guide to Florida outhouses with the hope that it will educate youngsters who never saw one, amuse those who grew up with one and maybe entertain anyone picking up the book in the privacy of their study or bathroom.

Outhouses used to be small structures that might fit in some of the more elegant bathrooms of today's houses. Those original ones did not usually have insulation, pictures on the walls or probably even any inside walls. The seat might be simply a plank of wood with one or more holes cut in it. The whole structure was placed over a deep pit in the ground.

"It may be true that a rolling stone gathers no moss, but a stationary outhouse certainly does."

This outhouse near Kingsley Lake outside Starke dates back to 1930. *Courtesy of James Flynn.*

Why the crescent and star on outhouses?

The crescent represents Luna, or "moon," and is the symbol for women. Its counterpart, the star or sunburst, represents men. Just as today we have ladies' rooms and men's rooms, outhouses were separated by gender. Today, though, it is the ladies' outhouse that is most often seen, as most male outhouses fell into disrepair.

These cutouts, usually above the line of sight, helped ventilate the structure and allowed the moonlight to shine in at night, which was safer than taking in a lit lantern.

This outhouse at Morningside Farm near Gainesville has a crescent and a star.

Wisdom from an old Floridian:

"If there's no outhouse in the woods, then you'll have to use a lavitree."

This outhouse near Citra was used as a storage shed.

Rules found in a Florida outhouse:

Refill catalogue and corncob box when empty.
Do not comment on the eating habits of other inhabitants.
Do not walk on seats.
Keep your shoes on.
No drinking or gambling.
Don't shoot any animals you find in the privy.

A modern outhouse, complete with a crescent, in Inverness.

An outhouse at Heritage Village in Largo. The sign on the side lists rules for using the facility.

This outhouse in Perry is wider than usual.

More rules found in a Florida outhouse:

If the outhouse is full, wait outside.

Those who have eaten refried beans or sauerkraut should use a neighbor's privy.

Knock once to determine if outhouse is occupied.

Knock twice for an emergency.

If you hear someone running on the path, get out quickly.

This modern, functioning outhouse is near Bland in northern Florida. *Courtesy of Henry Ebersole.*

"Today, the degradation of the inner life is symbolized by the fact that the only place sacred from interruption is the private toilet."
Lewis Mumford, U.S. social philosopher

This neat, well-maintained outhouse near Dade City is used to illustrate to schoolchildren how life was in the "good ole days."

An Ode to the Shack in the Back

"On the hole, thinking is great."

An old outhouse at Shiloh near Micanopy.

Many Floridians, especially the more daring men, tell stories of tipping over outhouses on Halloween. The idea was not to get caught, of course, and to tip one over while someone was inside deserved extra praise.

This former outhouse near Lake Louisa in Lake County beckons the motorists passing on U.S. 27.

A Tallahassee outhouse in 1950. *Courtesy of Florida State Archives.*

An Ode to the Shack in the Back

This combination structure near Lake Wales has an outdoor tub, a sink, a shower to the right of the sink and an outhouse to the right of that.

An Ode to the Shack in the Back

"There are the men who pretend to understand a book by scouting through the index; as if a traveler should go about to describe a place when he had seen nothing but the privy."

Jonathan Swift, *On the Mechanical Operation of the Spirit*

A leaning outhouse in Key West in the 1940s must have seen better days. *Courtesy of Florida State Archives.*

Two outhouses at Neighbor Guild Cooperative Colony near Lake Ashley in 1933.

Courtesy of Florida State Archives.

Another Halloween trick popular in many Florida towns was moving an outhouse to a strategic place, then adding creative signage. One outhouse in south Florida was frequently moved to the main street in town just outside a bank. The pranksters would then nail up a sign that read "Bank deposits here. Large and small deposits accepted at all hours."

To be locked

Seen on the back of a plumber's truck:
"In our business a flush beats a full house."

A crude sign inside this outhouse at the Marjorie Kinnan Rawlings state historic site warns visitors: "To be looked at, not sat at!"

The outside door of the Marjorie Kinnan Rawlings site outhouse has a wavy line.

This outhouse look-alike is actually a pump house near High Springs.

A north Floridian recalls once using hair spray near the outhouse. When the nozzle got stuck, she directed the spray into the john. Her husband followed her into the outhouse and had quite an "uplifting" experience when he threw his cigarette butt into the commode.

This outhouse near Lake Ashby in 1934 was neat and well constructed. *Courtesy of Florida State Archives.*

A post office in Drifton, Florida, with an outhouse out back in 1944 gave new meaning to the command about not dumping any mail. *Courtesy of Florida State Archives.*

An Ode to the Shack in the Back

A shy newlywed found that the house she and her husband were renting did not have a commode in the bathroom. In writing to the landlord, instead of writing "bathroom commode," she used the letters "B.C.," confident that he would understand what she meant.

When the landlord received the letter, at first he could not understand what the initials meant, but then guessed that they meant Baptist Church. He then answered her as follows:

Dear Ma'am:

I'm happy to tell you that we have a really nice B.C. about five miles down the road that will seat 300 people. Five miles might seem far, if you're in the habit of going regularly, but you'll be pleased to know that many people take their lunch and make a nice day of it.

When you arrive at the B.C., a handsome usher will take you to your seat and make sure you're comfortable. Years ago, men and women didn't sit together, but today we sit and meditate together.

It's a shame that many people around here don't go except on Mother's Day and Christmas. Even when they do go, they don't seem to do much. I hate to admit it, but I don't go as often as I should. As I get older, it takes more of an effort to go, especially in the cold weather.

Well, I hope to see you there real soon. If you want, I could come and go with you the first time, and introduce you to the others.

Sincerely,
Your landlord

Outhouses in Tampa were built by the Federal Emergency Relief Administration in 1935. *Courtesy of Florida State Archives.*

An Ode to the Shack in the Back

When Marjorie Kinnan Rawlings, Pulitzer Prize–winning author of *The Yearling*, moved to Cross Creek, Florida, in 1928, she inherited an outhouse on her new property. She remembered that her grandfather's outhouse was hidden away and had beautiful pictures of reigning European queens. Her new Florida outhouse, however, had no such décor. In fact, it stood directly opposite the dining room windows and did not even have a door, so that those sitting at the dining room table had an unpleasant view during dinner.

As she wrote in *Cross Creek*, the diners "could not lift their eyes from their plates without meeting the wooden stare of the unhappy and misplaced edifice. They were fortunate if they did not meet as well the eye of a belated occupant, assuring himself stonily that he could not be seen."

An outhouse in Columbia County. *Courtesy of Florida State Archives.*

A resident of north Florida recalls that, when she was young, her grandmother had once been using kerosene to remove the buildup of gum on her curtains that had come from the use of oil lamps. When she was finished cleaning, she tossed the kerosene into the outhouse, but neglected to tell Grandpa about this. He found out, however, when he lit his pipe in the outhouse and dropped the match into the hole. "Needless to say, he was defurred," the Floridian said.

This 1940s outhouse is on a dock at Garden Island, Florida. *Courtesy of Florida State Archives.*

This double outhouse in Tallahassee between two houses was used by seventeen families who lived in ten nearby houses. *Courtesy of Florida State Archives.*

Going into an outhouse in 1953 Bristol, Florida, a town considered by some as the original Garden of Eden. *Courtesy of Florida State Archives.*

In order to indicate whether her outhouse was occupied, Marjorie Kinnan Rawlings had a bright red, ragged quilt to place on the path to the structure. As she wrote in *Cross Creek*: "When one went in, one placed the flag in the path. When one came out, one put the flag back inside the outhouse." Heaven forbid that a person leaving the outhouse would forget to put the flag away, which occasionally happened.

This story was heard in north Florida near the Itchetucknee River. One Halloween night, young John Smith (the name is changed to protect the guilty) and his buddies decided to tip over the Smith privy and send it off into the Itchetucknee. They proceeded to do this, with a resulting crash into the river and many laughs over a job well done.

The next morning, John's dad pulled him out of bed, yanked him to his feet and demanded to know if John had been one of the boys who sent the outhouse into the river.

Remembering a history lesson about George Washington from school, young John proudly declared, "I cannot tell a lie. I was one of those boys who did it."

With that, his father proceeded to give him a spanking that John would long remember.

"But Pa," young John said. "When George Washington cut down the cherry tree and refused to tell a lie about it, his father was proud of him."

"Yes," John's father said. "But I betcha George's father was not *in* that cherry tree when he chopped it down."

This outhouse at the Dudley Farm near Newberry is a three-holer.

When Marjorie Kinnan Rawlings sold her first Florida story, "Jacob's Ladder," for the large sum of $700, she used the money to install indoor plumbing. But, as she wrote in *Cross Creek*, "I would not do anything so reckless as ordering a complete new bathroom outfit, but would shop around and pick up something second-hand."

The outhouse that stands at the Rawlings' house in Cross Creek hearkens back to a time when she was not quite "flush" with such royalties.

The corncobs inside the Dudley Farm outhouse represent an early form of toilet paper.

A privy at Tyner Farm in Laurel Hill, Florida, in 1992. *Courtesy of Florida State Archives.*

A 1944 outhouse in Tallahassee. *Courtesy of Florida State Archives.*

Should the door to the outhouse open inward or outward?

Argument for it opening inward: the person inside had better control of opening it, and it could open more quickly for someone racing down the path in an emergency. Disadvantage: opening it quickly could greatly disturb the person inside.

Argument for it opening outward: the door wouldn't have to fit exactly into the opening, it could be latched more easily and it could be kept open to enjoy the evening breezes. Disadvantage: for those who felt they could occasionally keep the door open, it would be just that time in the evening when someone would drive up with the lights on.

The Allentown School outhouse in 1990; this is north of Milton in the Florida panhandle. *Courtesy of Florida State Archives.*

This two-holer at the Green Light Service Station and restaurant complex in Beulah, Florida, was built around 1936 and used until the early 1950s. *Courtesy of Florida State Archives.*

From Jacksonville's *Florida Times-Union* (October 16, 1997): "Never underestimate the federal government's commitment to go first class with your money. It built an outhouse along a secluded hiking trail recently—for $333,000. Actually, the cost may have been $445,000, depending on whose records were more accurate, the contractor or the National Park Service."

Marjorie Kinnan Rawlings wrote in *Cross Creek* about the wire screen instead of a door on her outhouse: "For there was indeed a wire screen, and this screen had been, or so the instigator fatuously pretended, modernized with camouflage. Streaks of gray paint zigzagged across the screening."

Two dogs and a cat wait for their owner in San Felasco Hammock near Gainesville.

An Ode to the Shack in the Back

A privy at the Funston Mann farm in Baker County, Florida. *Courtesy of Florida State Archives.*

According to Willis Gertscsh's book *American Spiders* (1949), certain aggressive spiders hide in outhouses, partly because of the many flies found there that the spiders can eat. The spiders will spin their webs beneath the seats in the outhouse. Any disturbance of the delicate web will induce the spider to rush to the scene to bite the intruder as vigorously as possible. As quoted in the book, "Most victims of this type of black widow are males, and the injury is centered on the external genitalia."

These outhouses in Tallahassee are seen in a 1950 photograph. *Courtesy of Florida State Archives.*

The building of privies in Tampa in 1935. *Courtesy of Florida State Archives.*

A woman from Alachua recalls that when she was young and had only an outhouse at her cabin, a little neighbor boy once threw a rotten egg through the half-moon hole at the girl inside. She was splattered from head to foot. From then on, when one of the girls went to the john, another always stood guard outside.

A small house and privy someplace in Florida. *Courtesy of Florida State Archives.*

A Tallahassee outhouse in the 1940s. *Courtesy of Florida State Archives.*

This old outhouse in Apalachicola is tilting and becoming submerged in the weeds.

In place of toilet paper, which did not exist for many years, early Floridians used corncobs, newspapers or pages from catalogues. A woman once wrote to a particular catalogue company and ordered toilet paper. The company wrote back and asked for the page number and particular item number for her preferred toilet paper. She replied, "If I had the catalogue, I wouldn't need the toilet paper."

This leaning outhouse's days are numbered, as it sits near a planned $25 million complex in Cedar Key.

Florida Outhouses

The following story, related by a Gator grad, could just as well be used by students at other schools:

A particularly poor Gator fan asked a landlord about renting a room. "I don't have one in the main house," the landlord said, "but I have that old outhouse you can rent."

"Great," said the Gator fan. A month later the landlord asked the Gator fan how he was doing.

"Fine," said the Gator fan. "I fixed up the room really nice with some wallpaper and a nice chair. And to make a little extra money I've rented out the downstairs to a Seminole fan."

This outhouse in Windermere, Florida, is part of the only known example of a WPA-funded program in Orange County to provide outhouses in rural areas. *Courtesy of Florida State Archives.*

Two men in their twenties were using a two-holer near Tampa. When one of them finished and got up to go, a nickel fell out of his pants and down the hole. The man said, "Damn," and then dropped a ten-dollar bill down the hole. "What are you doing, buddy?" said the second.

"What do you think I'm doing? I don't want people to think I'd go down there for a lousy old nickel."

A house with an outdoor privy across from the Seaboard Station in Tallahassee in 1951. *Courtesy of Florida State Archives.*

What is an outhouse? It's a small house behind a big one, about one hundred yards away. In the wintertime, it's one hundred yards too far away. In the summertime, it's one hundred yards too close.

This privy was photographed in 1951 on Pinellas Street in Tallahassee. *Courtesy of Florida State Archives.*

This lonely outhouse near Lake Kissimmee has ventilation at the top.

A men's room in Lower Matecumbe Key in the Florida Keys in the 1940s. *Courtesy of the Farm Security Administration.*

Florida Outhouses

A writer complained in the *Tampa Tribune* (August 31, 1996) about the cost overruns of the stadium for the city's Tampa Bay Buccaneers. He used this headline: "Outhouses an option at stadium?" He pointed out that one county commissioner, in promising that the city would spend no more than $168 million, resolved, "I don't care if we have to build outhouses out there instead of toilets."

Two residences and the community outhouse in Tallahassee. *Courtesy of Florida State Archives.*

More rules for outhouses:
Men: raise the seat if not sitting.
Smokers and left-handers: sit to the left.
Not responsible for any newspapers or books left here.
Observe our four-page limit from the catalogue.
Don't discuss your condition with other occupants.
No fighting.

Part of this outhouse was for women ("HER'N") and part for men ("HIS'N") in Pahokee, Florida. *Courtesy of the Farm Security Administration.*

This double toilet was used by twenty-two families in Tallahassee. *Courtesy of Florida State Archives.*

A sawmill, seedling grove and nearby outhouse near DeLand around 1885. *Courtesy of Florida State Archives.*

When a resident of Gainesville lived in Alaska, he had an outhouse about forty feet from the main house. When he wanted to go to the outhouse, he would take a warmed toilet seat from the main house, go to the privy, use the toilet seat so as not to freeze his bottom to the cold wood and then return to the main house with the toilet seat. Once, as he opened the door to leave the outhouse, he found an angry moose right outside the door. The scared Floridian had to wait in the freezing outhouse until the moose finally ambled off.

Me on an outdoor privy in Ostia, near Rome, Italy. This structure is probably a thousand years old. *Courtesy of Karelisa Hartigan.*

"I wouldn't bet the farm on it, but I'd bet the main house. I wouldn't even bet the outhouse on Mondale."

President Richard Nixon on Ronald Reagan's chances of defeating Walter Mondale in the 1984 presidential election.

This original structure in a park in Barberville off Highway 40 has a stuffed figure inside that scares many an unsuspecting visitor.

Believe it or not, some archaeologists actually excavate outhouses. They do so in order to better understand life in previous times, since outhouses were often used as a convenient dumping ground for unwanted items like bottles, broken pottery, garden tools, even false teeth. Such outhouses, long since unused, have become totally dry and smell-free. Still, it takes a special person to become such an investigator.

A typical privy at the rear of a house in Tallahassee in 1951. *Courtesy of Florida State Archives.*

Houses and an old outhouse in Tallahassee in the 1940s. *Courtesy of Florida State Archives.*

About an outhouse with a flag:
"If the flag is at full-mast, it means that I'm inside with my pants at half-mast."

When Miami was incorporated in 1896, officials passed ordinances to govern life in the new settlement. Article 17, as passed on September 3, 1896, stated that the marshal shall see that all excrement from privies is removed as often as once in each week, or as often as may be required by the city council; he shall see that each privy in the corporate limits is provided by the owner or occupant with a bucket of the standard prescribed by the city council, the number of such buckets in any one privy to be regulated by the marshal, subject in case of dispute to the city council.

An old outhouse and a new one side by side in Polk County.

"Apollinaris medicus Titi imperatoris hic cacavit bene."

"Apollinaris, physician of the Emporor Titus, here shitted well."

Graffiti found on the wall of Herculaneum in Italy. This graffiti dates back to around AD 79, just before the eruption of Mount Vesuvius.

MY OUTHOUSE

During the second year of my stay in Turkey during my Peace Corps years (1963–65), this outhouse was my only bathroom at my home.

"Why am I here?"
Said by the author many times, especially at night in the pouring rain as he sat in his Turkish outhouse without any lights, radio or umbrella.

An Ode to the Shack in the Back

About the Author

Kevin McCarthy has been a professor of English and Florida Studies at the University of Florida for over thirty-one years. He was a Peace Corps volunteer in Turkey, a Fulbright scholar in Lebanon and Saudi Arabia and a student of Arabic in Cairo, Egypt.

He has had twenty-six books published on subjects ranging from sports, shipwrecks, pirates and English grammar. McCarthy teaches a college-level course on the Maritime History of Greece every other summer on the Greek island of Paros, and usually spends the month of May aboard cruise ships, lecturing about the languages, culture, history and literature of countries that border the Mediterranean.